Animal Eyes

By Connor Stratton

level
2
little blue
readers

www.littlebluehousebooks.com

Little Blue House is distributed by North Star Editions:
sales@northstareditions.com | 888-417-0195

Produced for Little Blue House by Red Line Editorial.

Photographs ©: iStockphoto, cover, 4, 6–7, 9, 11 (top), 11 (bottom), 12 (top), 15 (top), 15 (bottom), 17 (top), 17 (bottom), 18 (top), 18 (bottom), 20–21, 23, 24 (top left), 24 (top right), 24 (bottom left), 24 (bottom right); Shutterstock Images, 12 (bottom)

Library of Congress Control Number: 2020900789

ISBN
978-1-64619-175-8 (hardcover)
978-1-64619-209-0 (paperback)
978-1-64619-277-9 (ebook pdf)
978-1-64619-243-4 (hosted ebook)

Printed in the United States of America
Mankato, MN
082020

About the Author

Connor Stratton enjoys spotting new animals and writing books for children. He lives in Minnesota.

Table of Contents

Eyes All Around **5**

Shapes and
Colors **13**

Counting Eyes **19**

Glossary **24**

Index **24**

Eyes All Around

Many animals have eyes.

Eyes help animals see.

Fish have eyes.

Fish can see underwater.

Birds have eyes.

Birds can see from high in the sky.

Lizards have eyes.

Lions have eyes too.

eye

lizard

lion

eye

Shapes and Colors

Eyes can be

different shapes.

Some eyes are tall, and

some eyes are round.

Eyes can be
different colors.
Some eyes are red, and
some eyes are blue.

15

Some eyes are yellow,

and some eyes are green.

Counting Eyes

Many animals have

two eyes.

Monkeys have two eyes.

Dogs have two eyes too.

Some animals have more than two eyes. Spiders can have four eyes.

Some insects have

lots of eyes.

Flies can have thousands

of eyes.

fly

eyes

Glossary

fish

monkey

fly

spider

Index

D
dogs, 19

F
fish, 6

M
monkeys, 19

S
spiders, 20